Bayonet Fighting
for

BY

CAPTAIN LEOPOLD McLAGLEN

Inventor of the New System of Bayonet Fighting now used by British Troops in the Great War

30,000 ANZACS HAVE BEEN TRAINED IN THIS SYSTEM

WITH 55 ILLUSTRATIONS

PRICE **1/-** NET

LONDON
HARRISON AND SONS
Printers in Ordinary to His Majesty
Military Printers, Publishers and Stationers
ST. MARTIN'S LANE, W.C.

The Books you want—now

A PRACTICAL SERIES
BY PRACTICAL MEN

COMPLETE
CATALOGUE
POST FREE

MILITARY DEPARTMENT
HARRISON & SONS
Printers in Ordinary to His Majesty
ST. MARTIN'S LANE, LONDON, W.C.

**WIDELY ADOPTED THROUGHOUT
THE NEW ARMIES &
VOLUNTEER TRAINING CORPS**

MILITARY PUBLICATIONS

Swedish Drill Illustrated

The Maxim of the Moment
GET FIT!

FOR
Recruit Squads, Volunteer Training Corps, Lads' Brigades, Scouts, Senior Boys' Classes, and for Home Use

Written and illustrated by Experts. Plain, Simple and Concise

PRICE —/6 NET

POST FREE SEVENPENCE

Recruit Training (Infantry) 1914

An aid to all Instructors

NET —/6 NET

POST FREE SEVENPENCE

WIDELY USED THROUGHOUT THE NEW ARMIES

"A very useful little book: send me by return 100 copies."
—COMM. OFFICER, —TH BN. —— REGT.

"Please forward at once 250 copies to O.C. —rd Bn. —— Regt."
—CAPT. AND ADJT.

FIRST EDITION SOLD OUT IN THREE WEEKS

ADOPTED BY COMMANDERS EVERYWHERE

Handbook for Company Officers

A Valuable Aid

HANDY SIZE 1/6 CLOTH BOUND

POST FREE 1/9

180 Pages. 18 Whole Page Illustrations

"This convenient and well-arranged handbook sets out in clear and simple language an epitome of the duties which fall to a company officer and a group leader."

". . . The Handbook should certainly supply a want . . . should prove useful to all ranks and to all arms."

SHOULD BE READ BY ALL OFFICERS & N.C.Os.

Physical Drill for Home Defence Corps

WITH ILLUSTRATIONS & SPECIMEN LESSONS

PRICE —/6 NET

POST FREE SEVENPENCE

MILITARY PUBLICATIONS

Squad Drill Illustrated

Practically Written
Graphically Depicted

Including

SECTION DRILL RIFLE EXERCISES
PLATOON DRILL EXTENDED ORDER

Can be understood by anybody

PRICE –/6 NET

Post Free Sevenpence

Company Drill Illustrated

(IN RED COVER)

Illustrating clearly each movement as laid down in "Infantry Training, 1914," and showing the positions of platoon and section commanders

THE NEXT BOOK TO "SQUAD DRILL"

PRICE –/6 NET

Post Free Sevenpence

Battalion Drill Illustrated

Indispensable to Officers and N.C.Os.

Full of Graphic Illustrations

Depicted with great clarity both in the letterpress and accompanying sketches

A wealth of detail invaluable to all who are in command of Units of any denomination

PRICE 1/– NET

Post 1/1 Free

MILITARY PUBLICATIONS

Duties for all Ranks
A Compendium of Information

From the C.O. to the Private

SPECIALLY COMPILED FOR THE

NEW ARMIES & VOLUNTEER TRAINING CORPS

Clear and concise, embracing
Adjutant's Duties. Officers' Messes

Every Officer, N.C.O. and Private should have a' copy of this Manual

A GUIDE FOR ALL

PRICE —/6 NET

Post Free Sevenpence

From the Front: Notes for the New Armies

Written from Personal Experience

FULL OF VALUABLE HINTS

Much can be learnt from this book which will prove extremely serviceable

PRICE —/6 NET

Post Free Sevenpence

Guard Duty Illustrated

DIRECT—SIMPLE—USEFUL
FULL OF INFORMATION

Invaluable alike to the Regulars Territorials and the V.T.C.

All you want to know about Guard Duties

PRICE —/6 NET

Post Free Sevenpence

Bayonet Fighting for War

BY

CAPTAIN LEOPOLD McLAGLEN

Inventor of the New System of Bayonet Fighting now used by British Troops in the Great War

30,000 ANZACS HAVE BEEN TRAINED IN THIS SYSTEM

WITH 55 ILLUSTRATIONS

LONDON
HARRISON AND SONS
Printers in Ordinary to His Majesty
Military Printers, Publishers and Stationers
ST. MARTIN'S LANE, W.C.

Captain Leopold McLaglen.

The McLaglen System of Bayonet Fighting.

Death-dealing Science Imparted to our Soldiers.

From " *The Weekly Press*," Christchurch, N.Z., June 30th, 1915.

CAPTAIN LEOPOLD McLAGLEN, the inventor of the McLaglen System of Bayonet Fighting, which has revolutionised the old-fashioned theory concerning the use of this weapon, had a very interesting chat with a representative of this journal last week.

" Before and after the Boer War," said Captain McLaglen, " many leading military experts declared that the bayonet, as a weapon, had practically ceased to exist or to fulfil any useful purpose. But this huge world's war has been responsible for the tearing down of many old ideas and the raising up of new ones. Field-Marshal Sir John French, the greatest cavalry leader of the British Army, admits that infantry is undoubtedly the queen of battle. Now the British infantryman has always proved himself an adept with the bayonet at all times. This was proved under Wellington in the Pyrenees, proved at Waterloo, proved particularly at Inkerman, and proved time and again in the Indian Mutiny, and in all the different frontier and other campaigns Britain has had to wage in the East."

" But," asked the reporter, " has not the invention of modern guns and heavy field artillery made some difference to this ? "

" In opinion, yes," was the reply, "since the invention of modern artillery it has been intimated on the highest military authority that warfare would be conducted in future at long range. This war proves the absolute falsity of that as a complete statement of the case. Little did military experts think that a great modern war would turn into siege warfare where so many entrenchments are absolutely essential for the protection of the fighting line. The close proximity of these trenches gives the opportunities for the use of the bayonet that have been so effectively described in recent letters from men at the Front. After heavy artillery support, the infantrymen spring from their trenches over a distance of between 200 to 500 yards, and charge the enemy with the bayonet. Very often the enemy spring from their trenches to meet the British infantrymen, but we have not yet received information that any British regiment has ever lost out in a bayonet combat with the enemy. Therefore it has been proved to the instructional staffs that the knowledge of the use of the bayonet is just as important as other branches of military training, and it is absolutely essential that all men going to this war should have a thorough and complete knowledge of the use of this weapon."

"The usefulness was particularly proved, was it not, at the Dardanelles with our own men?" queried the reporter.

"It was, indeed," emphatically replied the Captain. "There is no doubt whatever that the success which the British and Australasian troops attained was due in very large measure to the instruction which they had received in the McLaglen system of bayonet fighting. It is impossible to deny the effectiveness of that method. It is in use now with the Home armies, and I have trained more than 30,000 Australasian troops. I trained the New Zealand Expeditionary Forces at Trentham, and have left behind me there competent instructors to carry on the work. I have been attached to the Central Administration of Australia, but am spending some little time in New Zealand training as many men as I possibly can," explained Captain McLaglen.

"Would you mind giving a general outline of your system of bayonet fighting?"

"I invented this some five years ago. After carefully studying the system in vogue in the British Army, the French Army, the Russian Army, and the Japanese Army, I came to the conclusion that these systems did not get the full effect that can be got out of the rifle and bayonet. Each system was incomplete, and in consequence I set to work to invent a complete system, and it has absolutely revolutionised all the methods previously in vogue. It teaches us that a comparatively small man with a knowledge of this new system is more than an equal match for an opponent without it, though three or four times his own weight and physical strength. Military authorities who have seen the system have at once realised its immense importance and value, and in every case after demonstration it has been chosen to supersede the old obsolete methods. It is a system which when once demonstrated to any military officer proves its own value immediately. It is absolutely thorough and absolutely complete. It is impossible to get any more work out of a rifle and bayonet than is got out of this new system. At close-quarter bayonet fighting, when the different points in this new system are delivered, it is impossible to guard any one of the points; at the same time the defence is so thorough as to completely neutralise your opponent's efforts. Every contingency is provided for; every point of vantage on the enemy is taken. Should a man ever fall and lose his rifle, or be partially disabled and lose it, instead of being at his opponent's mercy, he is still as dangerous as ever, and the system provides a means whereby in an incredibly short space of time the positions are reversed by throwing your opponent and taking his rifle and leaving him defenceless."

"In this new system of bayonet fighting there is a certain amount of jiu-jitsu, and as the authorities are now enlisting bantam battalions, these bantam battalions are being trained in the rudiments of jiu-jitsu. This will undoubtedly give these small men more confidence in themselves to attack larger and more powerful men. We ofttimes hear of the pen being mightier than the sword, although it is a much smaller weapon. Jiu-jitsu teaches us that the small and apparently weak man must not always be despised. Jiu-jitsu undoubtedly overcomes brute force and physical strength. Therefore the knowledge of jiu-jitsu introduced into the McLaglen System of Bayonet Fighting adds greatly to the value of the system as a whole. This is being realised more and more every day by the military authorities, and a knowledge of jiu-jitsu will soon become an integral part of the training we give to our soldiers before they go to the Front."

Testimonials.

Testimonials have been received from the following Officers, which bear testimony to the effectiveness of the new points added to the System of Bayonet Fighting used in the British Army.

Captain L. McLaglen has instructed 20,000 men of the 1st and 2nd Expeditionary Force of Australia in this new system of bayonet fighting, and testimonials have been received, amongst others, from the following :—

> General R. LEGGE, G.O.C. Australian Forces.
> Major F. DARVALL, Hd.-Qrs., Broadmeadows.
> Lieut.-Col. A. J. V. WHITE, O.C. 8th Light Horse Regiment.
> Col. J. M. ARNOTT, O.C. 7th Light Horse Regiment.

10,000 men have been instructed in New Zealand from this new system :—

> Brig.-General A. M. ROBIN, Commanding New Zealand Military Force.
> Sir Joseph G. WARD, N.Z.
> Col. GIBBON, Chief of General Staff, N.Z.
> Lieut.-Col. G. W. MACDONALD.

"I consider his system far superior to the ordinary method of bayonet fighting, and can confidently recommend it."

> Lieut.-Col. HUNTER MACANDREW, O.C. South Island Battalion, N.Z.R.E.

"Your system of bayonet fighting was a revelation to me, and I was surprised at the efficiency of your class at the termination of your training."

Lieut.-Col. J. MURPHY, O.C. 1st Canterbury Regiment, N.Z.

" It was, to my mind, marvellous that at the end of eight nights' instruction the men were able to give such a fine display at the assault-at-arms."

Col. R. O. CHAFFEY, Comdg. Canterbury Military District, N.Z.

" I consider his style of teaching, and the results, most satisfactory."

Major L. REYNELL, O.C. 9th Light Horse, A.I.F.

" The men have learnt increased confidence in their ability to use their weapons."

Our practical teaching under Captain McLaglen's system (Captain McLaglen was our Staff Bayonet Instructor at Broadmeadows, Victoria, Australia) stood us in good stead at Gaba Tepe when the Turks charged our trenches in June, 1915.

Our men, the 9th Light Horse, sprang from their trenches and met the Turks on open ground, Every man had by his previous training a thorough confidence in his bayonet, and the lessons learned were put to good use. The enemy were routed with tremendous loss to them, our men mowing through them with the bayonet. Our casualties only amounted to about half a dozen at the outside.

(Signed)   L. H. SWANN,
            Late 9th Light Horse, A.I.F.,
            Lieut. 2/1st Suffolk Yeomanry.

The first Victoria Cross won by the Australian Forces in the Dardanelles has brought with it a testimonial to the system of bayonet fighting which was invented by Captain McLaglen.

Lance-Corporal Albert Jacka, who has been awarded the V.C., received the decoration as a result of his having killed seven Turks single-handed, five with the rifle and two with the bayonet. Lance-Corporal Jacka was one of the original squad trained in the McLaglen system,

Method of Instruction.

The best results in training troops in the McLaglen System of Bayonet Fighting can be gained by using the following methods:—

By forming a company in two squares, one square inside the other, as follows :—

The men forming the squares to be three paces distant apart, the inner square to be termed the front rank, the outer square the rear rank. The instructor stands in the centre. Both ranks face inwards during the preliminary instruction in parry and point.

After the men have become efficient in parry and point the instructor will then commence teaching close quarter fighting. The instructor must now have the assistance of another to demonstrate. After demonstrating to all sides of the square the movement to be performed, the instructor will give the order for the inner rank to "About Turn" which brings the front and rear ranks covering and facing one another. The men will stand at "Attention."

Orders will now be given by whistle blast.

On the first blast both front and rear ranks will spring to the "On Guard" position, stepping forward on the left foot.

Whistle: Both front and rear ranks will deliver the "High Right Parry," "Point," "On Guard," in quick time.

Whistle: "Low Right Parry," "Point," "On Guard."

Whistle: "High Left Parry," "Point," "On Guard."

Whistle: "Low Left Parry," "Point," "On Guard."

Whistle: Both front and rear ranks will advance towards one another and "Cross Rifles."

Whistle: Front rank will deliver "Right Hook to Jaw," and recover.

Whistle: Rear rank will deliver " Right Hook to Jaw," and recover.
Whistle: Both ranks recover original positions and spring to " Attention."
Whistle: Both ranks come to " On Guard."

Before proceeding to close quarter fighting, in **each** case, the instructor should put the men through the parries and points as given above.

The succeeding positions are carried out in similar fashion, as explained above.

Men: Three paces apart.   Ranks: Six paces apart.

Descriptive.

1. Captain McLaglen on left, Major Finnis on right.
2. On Guard.
3. Same as 2, but different position, showing detail.
   Right elbow on butt, right hand on small, left hand just below centre band, right and left knees bent.
4. Right High Parry.
5. Right Low Parry.
6. Left High Parry.
7. Left Low Parry.
8. Point to Opponent's Breast.
9. Right Hook to Jaw.
   Failing to get your point in on opponent, and your opponent closing in on you, rifles crossing at close quarters, you immediately resort to right hook blow to jaw. In this position the body is protected from opponent's rifle and bayonet by keeping left hand grip on rifle slightly out from left shoulder.
10. Knuckle and Elbow Blow.
    From close quarter position when rifles are crossed; by forcing opponent's rifle with your rifle by a quick movement to your opponent's left, immediately changing position, delivering blow to opponent's knuckle, so that the magazine strikes his knuckles and the toe of the butt his elbow. It is impossible for your opponent to escape from this blow, which must incapacitate him.
11. Same as 10, showing detail.

12. Solar Plexus Blow.
When in close quarters with opponent, and it is too dangerous to shorten arms to deliver a "point," resort at once to a right hook blow on solar plexus. It is important that the left hand grip on rifle should be kept well in front of the body, the head being immediately behind and thus covered by rifle.

13. Rio Blow.
An effective blow in close quarters. Stepping smartly forward with left foot, left knee well bent, deliver blow with butt of rifle to opponent's lower part.

14. Rio Blow.
Same as Fig. 13, showing detail (figures reversed).

15. Upper Cut to Jaw.
Your point being parried by opponent coming into close quarters, step smartly forward on left foot, swinging rifle in an upper cut blow to jaw, right arm to full extent, left hand grip on rifle in line with left ear.

16. Recovering Failure in 15—Blow to Head.
Failing to deliver blow to opponent's jaw (see Fig. 15) and your opponent pulling his rifle downwards endeavouring to guard your blow, you immediately resort to a quarter staff blow to head by reversing your position and bringing the rifle forward with left hand smartly. The fact of your opponent guarding blow to jaw will materially increase the speed of your movement.

17. Upper Cut.

18. Head.

19. Neck and Trip.
When at close quarters with opponent his equilibrium may be readily upset, thus placing you in position to deliver "Point." From the cross rifle position force opponent's rifle to his left, dropping your bayonet on side of opponent's neck, your opponent naturally flinches to the right, his rifle being locked by your movement and your own body being

guarded. At this moment place your left foot at the side of opponent's left foot, trip his left foot smartly to the left, at the same time forcing your bayonet downwards on opponent's neck. This will result in a fall to your enemy, when immediately shorten arms to put him out of action. It must be thoroughly understood that it requires a certain amount of force and power at the back of a "point" before it will put a man out of action. It must be borne in mind that the bayonet has to penetrate a thick tunic and possibly several layers of under garments before injury can be done.

20. **Throw from Neck and Trip—Shorten Arms.**
21. **Neck and Trip.**
22. **Shorten Arms.**
23. **Cross Buttock.**
    From close quarters when struggling for supremacy and too dangerous to shorten arms, turn half-right with your body and place your left leg at the back of opponent's left leg, simultaneously placing your rifle across his chest and rifle, forcing same downwards with your left hand, and kicking your left leg backwards. Follow up the resultant fall by delivering "point."
24. **Cross Buttock.**
25. **Shorten Arms.**
26. **Rifle Lost. Struggle ensues for Opponent's Rifle.**
    It is possible that a man may drop his rifle or even be in a better position by voluntarily relinquishing it and grasping his opponent's rifle, which should be done in this way. Seize the rifle, left hand knuckles upwards, right hand knuckles downwards. Immediately close your grip on opponent's left hand, your left hand encircling his knuckles, thumb well at back of his hand, your right hand fingers encircling opponent's butt of thumb with your thumb at back of his knuckle. Stepping smartly back at the same moment bend your opponent's wrist towards himself in a sharp jerk to his left, forcing downwards.

27. Position of Hands when taking Opponent's Rifle.
28. Position of Hands when taking Opponent's Rifle.
29. Opponent thrown from Jiu-jitsu Grip.
    Opponent is now thrown, but perhaps retains his grip on rifle. Bring your left shin bone against his left elbow, and continue the grip and twist as before, forcing his elbow forward with your left knee, your antagonist will release his grasp; recover rifle and deliver " point." From positions as described in Figs. 26, 27 and 28, it is possible to take a revolver, knife, or any other object, or, in a hand to hand conflict without weapons, to incapacitate an opponent.
30. Intense Pain causes Opponent to Release Grasp of Rifle.
31. Opponent being put out of Action with his own Weapon.
32. Un-armed, but still Dangerous—The Leg-throw.
    Should the positions be reversed and you have been thrown, as in Fig. 32, with your opponent about to despatch you, place your left foot at the back of his left foot, and your right foot on opponent's knee; kick or push smartly with right foot, at the same time drawing left foot forward. This will throw your opponent. Immediately grasp him by his foot (Fig. 33), left hand encircling his instep, right hand encircling his heel; twist opponent's foot sharply inwards, turning him on to his face (Fig. 34). Place your right foot into the bend of his leg, still retaining the grip on his toes, and force his foot downwards towards his body (Fig. 35).
33. Thrown—Preparing for the Leg Lock.
34. About to apply Leg Lock.
35. The Lock applied—Taking Opponent's Rifle.
36. Rio Kick.
    Should the position as just described be reversed the rio kick as above can be used either as a counter to your opponent's movement or as a means of attack. Bring the knees smartly up opponent's lower parts.

2.—EN GARDE.

2.—On Guard.

1.—CAPT. MCLAGLEN À GAUCHE, MAJOR FINNIS À DROITE.

1.—Capt. McLaglen on left, Major Finnis on right.

3.—LE MÊME QUE 2, MAIS POSITION DIFFÉRENTE, MONTRANT LE DÉTAIL.

3.—Same as 2, but different position, showing detail.

5.—PARÉ DROIT BAS.

5.—Right Low Parry.

4.—PARÉ DROIT HAUT.

4.—Right High Parry.

6.—PARÉ GAUCHE HAUT.

7.—PARÉ GAUCHE BAS.

6.—Left High Parry.

7.—Left Low Parry.

8.—POINTE À LA POITRINE DE L'ADVERSAIRE.

8.—Point to Opponent's Breast.

9.—CROCHET DROIT À LA MÂCHOIRE.

10.—COUP DE JOINTURE ET COUDE.

9.—Right Hook to Jaw.

10.—Knuckle and Elbow Blow.

11.—LE MÊME QUE 10, MONTRANT LE DÉTAIL.

12.—COUP SOLAR PLEXUS.

11.—Same as 10, showing detail.

12.—Solar Plexus Blow.

13.—COUP RIO.

14.—COUP RIO.

13. Rio Blow.

14.—Rio Blow.

16.—REPRISE APRÈS L'ÉCHEC EN 15 : COUP À LA TÊTE.

16.—Recovering Failure in 15 : Blow to Head.

15.—COUP EN HAUT À LA MÂCHOIRE.

15.—Upper Cut to Jaw.

17.—COUP EN HAUT.

17.—Upper Cut.

18.—TÊTE.　　18.—Head.

19.—COU ET CROC-EN-JAMBE.

20.—TERRASSÉ PAR COU ET CROC-EN-JAMBE ; ARMES RACCOURCIES.

19.—Neck and Trip.

20.—Throw from Neck and Trip: shorten arms.

21.—COU ET CROC-EN-JAMBE.

22.—ARMES RACCOURCIES.

21.—Neck and Trip.

22.—Shorten Arms.

23.—CROC-EN-JAMBE.

23.—Cross Buttock.

24.—CROC-EN-JAMBE.

24.—Cross Buttock.

25.—ARMES RACCOURCIES

25.—Shorten Arms.

26.—FUSIL PERDU: LUTTE POUR OBTENIR LE FUSIL DE L'ADVERSAIRE.

26.—Rifle Lost: struggle ensues for opponent's rifle.

23.—POSITION DES MAINS EN S'EMPARANT DU FUSIL DE L'ADVERSAIRE.

28.—Position of Hands when taking Opponent's Rifle.

27.—POSITION DES MAINS EN S'EMPARANT DU FUSIL DE L'ADVERSAIRE.

27.—Position of Hands when taking Opponent's Rifle.

29.—L'ADVERSAIRE TERRASSÉ PAR UNE PRISE JIÛ JITSU.

30.—DOULEUR INTENSE QUI OBLIGE L'ADVERSAIRE À LÂCHER SON FUSIL.

29.—Opponent Thrown from Jiu-Jitsu Grip.

30. Intense Pain causes Opponent to Release Grasp of Rifle.

32.—DÉSARMÉ, MAIS ENCORE DANGEREUX. CHUTE CAUSÉE PAR LES JAMBES.

32.—Unarmed, but still dangerous: The Leg Throw.

31.—L'ADVERSAIRE EN TRAIN D'ÊTRE MIS HORS DE COMBAT PAR SA PROPRE ARME.

31.—Opponent being put out of Action with his own weapon.

33.—TERRASSÉ: PRÉPARATOIRE AVANT DE SERRER LA JAMBE.

33.—Thrown: Preparing for the leg-lock.

34.—SUR LE POINT DE SERRER LA JAMBE.

34.—About to Apply Leg-lock.

35.—LA PRISE TERMINÉE : S'EMPARANT DU FUSIL DE L'ADVERSAIRE.

36.—COUP DE GENOU RIO.

35.—The Lock Applied : taking opponent's rifle.

36.—Rio Kick.

MOUNTED BAYONET FIGHTING

Mounted Bayonet Fighting.

PRELIMINARY TRAINING.

The training a recruit must undergo to become efficient in mounted bayonet fighting must first be started by learning the various positions dismounted, with legs apart as if astride a horse.

1. **From the Position " Carry Arms."**
2. **" Engage."**
    Dropping butt of rifle smartly under right armpit, bayonet point to the front in line with the right shoulder.
3. **To the Right " Point " at Infantry.**
    Turning body smartly to the half-right, legs in same position as Fig. 1, pointing bayonet forward to the right-front at about the height of an infantryman's chest, with the butt of the rifle resting under the right fore-arm.
4. **To the Right " Point " at Infantry.**
5. **To the Right " Point " at Cavalry.**
    Turning body smartly to the half-right, legs in same position as Fig. 1, pointing bayonet forward to the right-front at about the height of a cavalryman's chest, with the butt of the rifle resting under the right fore-arm.
6. **To the Right " Point " at Cavalry.**
7. **To the Left " Point " at Infantry.**
    From the " Engage " (Fig. 2) raise rifle in a circular movement over horse's head, pointing to the left to Infantry. In all cases butt of rifle must rest under right fore-arm.
8. **To the Left " Point " at Infantry.**
9. **To the Left " Point " at Cavalry.**
10. **To the Left " Point " at Cavalry.**
    From the " Engage " (Fig. 2) raise rifle in a circular movement over horse's head, pointing to the left to Cavalry. In all cases butt of rifle must rest under right fore-arm.

1.—DE LA POSITION "PORTEZ ARMES."   2.—"ENGAGE."

1.—From the Position "Carry Arms."   2.—"Engâge."

3.—À LA DROITE "POINTE" À L'INFANTERIE.

3.—To the right "Point" at Infantry.

4.—À LA DROITE "POINTE" À L'INFANTERIE.

4.—To the right "Point" at Infantry.

5.—À LA DROITE "POINTE" À LA CAVALERIE.

5.—To the right "Point" at Cavalry.

6.—À LA DROITE "POINTE" À LA CAVALERIE.

6.—To the right "Point" at Cavalry.

7.—À LA GAUCHE "POINTE" À L'INFANTERIE.

7.—To the left "Point" at Infantry.

8.—À LA GAUCHE "POINTE" À L'INFANTERIE.

8.—To the left "Point" at Infantry.

9.—À LA GAUCHE "POINTE" À LA CAVALERIE.

9.—To the left "Point" at Cavalry.

10.—À LA GAUCHE "POINTE" À LA CAVALERIE.

10.—To the left "Point" at Cavalry.

11.—DE LA POSITION "PORTEZ ARMES."

12.—"ENGAGE."

11.—From the Position "Carry Arms."

12.—"Engage."

13.—À LA DROITE "POINTE" À L'INFANTERIE.

13.—To the right "Point" at Infantry.

14.—À LA DROITE "POINTE" À LA CAVALERIE.

14.—To the right "Point" at Cavalry.

15.—À LA GAUCHE "POINTE" À L'INFANTERIE.

15.—To the left "Point" at Infantry.

16.—À LA GAUCHE "POINTE" À LA CAVALERIE.

16.—To the left "Point" at Cavalry.

Katsu Resuscitation.

Katsu, the Japanese system of resuscitation, was known, according to authentic records, 200 years B.C. These records are in the possession of the Mikado of Japan. Especially reticent are the Japanese regarding a dozen or two death-producing grips and blows; some of these have been described in detail, others only hinted at. The death blows are remarkable; some are delivered on the spine, others on the head (two on the face). When the victim of one of these deadly touches does not regain consciousness in a short time, and the heart's action and the breathing reach such a low point that death may ensue, it is then time to resort to the secret science of Katsu. This is applied on certain nerve centres, and by pressure stimulates those nerves and causes a reaction of the heart. The nerves affected are those of the pectoral arch, where the thinness of the tissues and other matter leaves the nerve most exposed. Two other centres that are affected simultaneously are the pneumogastric centre and the auditory nerves of the brain. It is possible to restore a man to life who has fallen dead through disordered action of the heart, and in a fainting or epileptic fit to restore the patient to his normal condition in a few seconds. Many soldiers in warfare die through a bullet entering their body. It is not necessary that the bullet struck a vital part, but they die through shock. In such cases it is possible to restore the dead by the science of Katsu.

1ᵉ POSITION.

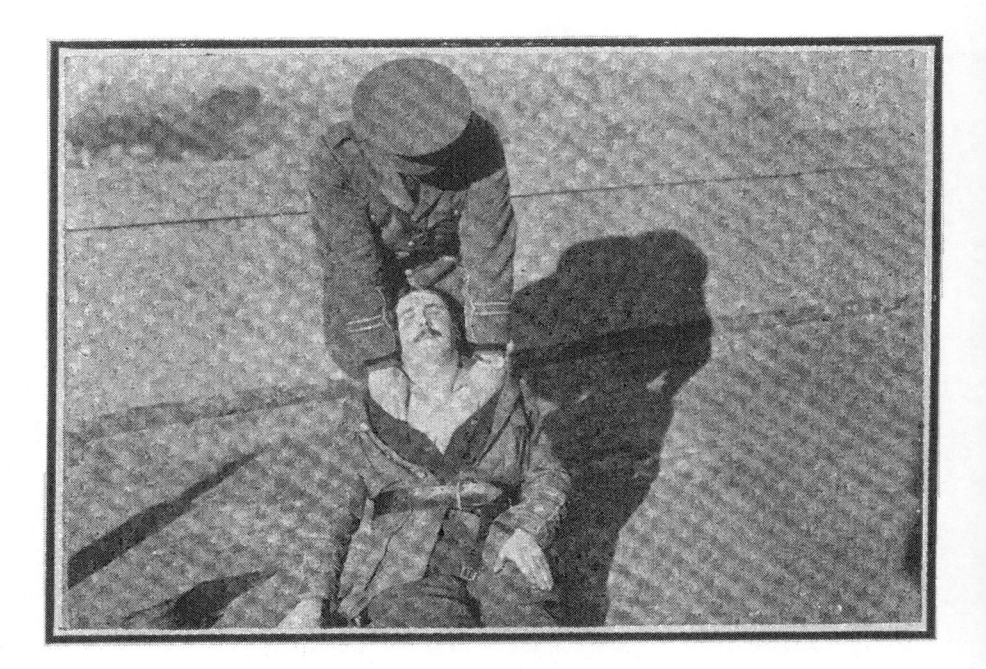

Position I.

The restorer, supporting the patient with left knee, places his thumbs in the hollows of the pectoral arch, and applies pressure by the fingers, with upward and downward movement of the whole hand.

2ᵉ POSITION.

Position II.

Left knee supporting patient, right knee retracted.

Position III.

Right knee delivering a light blow upon or about the seventh vertebra. The effect of this shock, which is transmitted to the pneumogastric nerve, and is applied after the pressure of the fingers upon the pectoral nerve centre, and with a simultaneous shout into the patient's ear (which stimulates the auditory nerve), is to restore the apparently dead man to life. Katsu will be of especial value to medical men, for it will avail against the collapse of a patient after operation, or in syncope after administration of an anæsthetic.

MILITARY PUBLICATIONS

Rifle Shooting for War
A Practical Illustrated Book

The outcome of the experience of an International Rifleman

SIMPLE—USEFUL—PRACTICAL
For Teachers and Self-Instruction

PRICE —/6 NET
Post Free Sevenpence

INVALUABLE FOR MUSKETRY EVERYWHERE

Fire Orders Direction & Control

A Supplement to "Rifle Shooting for War"

MUSKETRY IN ITS ADVANCED FORM

PRICE —/6 NET
Post Free Sevenpence

Aids to Musketry

A Valuable Manual on an Important Subject

USEFUL ALIKE TO THE NEW ARMIES & V.T.C.

PRICE —/6 NET
Post Free Sevenpence

Maze Drill Illustrated

A Valuable Adjunct for Training
Increasing Smartness and Stamina

PRICE 1/— NET
Post 1/2 Free

MILITARY PUBLICATIONS

Company & Platoon Commands

A Pocket Aid to Memory

PRICE **3d.** NET

Post -/3½ Free

SMALL—COMPACT—CONCISE

Automatic Pistols & Revolvers

Every Officer should peruse this little work before purchasing the weapon upon which his life may depend

THE VARIOUS MODELS FULLY ILLUSTRATED AND DESCRIBED

PRICE **-/6** NET

Post Free Sevenpence

Artillery Field Formulæ

For 18-pr. and 15-pr. B.L.C.

All the necessary Data at a Glance

COMPACT FOR THE POCKET
PRINTED ON LINEN

PRICE **-/6** NET

Post Free Sevenpence

Infantry Range-Finder

Compact and Useful

PRICE **2d.** PRICE

Post -/2½ Free

MILITARY PUBLICATIONS

English—Flemish Military Guide

Wholly elaborated close to the line of battle, where the first editions have also been printed and sold

PRICE **10d.** NET
Post 1/- Free

Invaluable to all Troops proceeding to Flanders

Military Guide to the Dardanelles & Eastern Campaign

WITH
FIELD VOCABULARY
IN
English—French—Greek—Turkish

PRICE **2/6** NET
Post 2/9 Free

English—French Guides & Vade-Mecums

Full List Post Free

Canvas and Camaraderie

A Charming Souvenir for your Friends

FULLY ILLUSTRATED

"The authors have contrived a delightfully written and often amusing book." "Clearly shows the genuine comradeship of the life." "Should revive pleasant memories." "Its smartness is undeniable." "Should prove a blessing in every camp, the collection of songs being most interesting." *Vide* Press.

PRICE **—/6** NET
Post Free Sevenpence

Field States British Expeditionary Force

AND OTHER DATA

PRICE **1/—** NET
Post 1/1 Free

"A mass of data; strength, road space, animals, transport, tools, medical services, bridging material, camp billets, etc.; of great value for quick reference."

HARRISON & SONS

Regimental Journals, Magazines, Histories, Standing Orders, Printed and Published

LETTERPRESS
LITHOGRAPHY
BOOKBINDING
STATIONERY
BLOCK - MAKING
DIE STAMPING
ENGRAVING
PUBLISHING
MUSIC PRINTING
&c. &c. &c.

MILITARY DEPARTMENT
Correspondence Invited

Recruiting Posters, Booklets, &c., Designed and Executed

Printers in Ordinary to His Majesty and to Queen Alexandra
Military Printers, Publishers and Stationers
ST. MARTIN'S LANE, LONDON, W.C.

THREE NEW BOOKS

PLATOON AND COMPANY DRILL

FULLY ILLUSTRATED

Compiled by the Commandant and Officers on the Staff of the London District School of Instruction

The Official Manual of the School

PRICE 1/-

Post 1/1 Free

THE LAST WORD IN DRILL BOOKS

KNOWLEDGE FOR WAR

Every Officer's Handbook for the Front

ILLUSTRATED. POCKET SIZE

Expert Information on every subject which an Officer must know before being selected

FOR SERVICE IN THE FIELD

Discipline—Drill—Musketry—Tactics and Field Warfare—Topography—Trench Warfare—Billeting—Machine Guns—Interior Economy and Military Law—Physical Drill—Signalling

By CAPTAIN B. C. LAKE

King's Own Scottish Borderers

Supervising Officer of Officers' Training Class, 7th (R) Brigade

PRICE 2/6

Post 2/9 Free

MACHINE GUN MANUAL

By LIEUT. H. DOUGLAS

Sherwood Foresters

National Team (England); Kolapore Team (Great Britain) British Rifle Team (Australian Tour)

MAXIM—VICKERS—LEWIS AUTOMATIC—COLT

FULLY ILLUSTRATED

PRICE 1/-

Post 1/2 Free

WRIGHT'S
Coal Tar
SHAVING SOAP
the Ideal Shaving Soap for Soldiers.

It has all the hygienic properties of WRIGHT'S Coal Tar Soap as well as its clean, wholesome smell. Protects the skin from every form of "rash" and gives a persistent creamy, but not slimy lather.

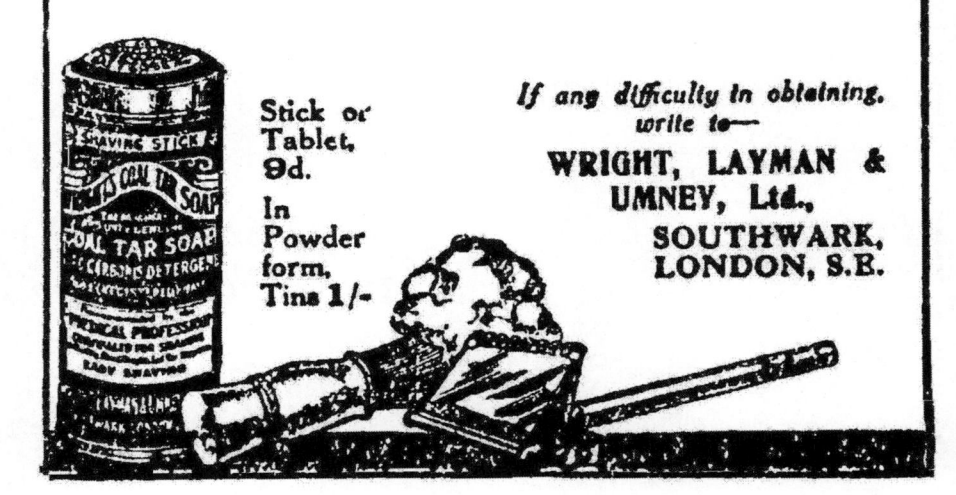

Stick or Tablet, 9d.
In Powder form, Tins 1/-

If any difficulty in obtaining, write to—
WRIGHT, LAYMAN & UMNEY, Ltd., SOUTHWARK, LONDON, S.E.

Printed in Great Britain
by Amazon